HET NUMMER VERHAAL

THE NUMBER STORY

SMALL BOOK ONE

ENGLISH - DUTCH

*Numbers Teach Children
Their Number Names*

written and illustrated by

MISS ANNA

Early Reader Edition of *The Number Story 1*
Bronze Medal Winner, 2016 Wishing Shelf Book Award

Library of Congress Control Number: 2018902040

Names: Miss Anna, author.
Title: Number story : numbers teach children their number names / Miss Anna.
Description: Portland, OR: Lumpy Publishing, 2018.
Identifiers: ISBN 978-1-945977-42-8 | LCCN 2018902040
Summary: The pictures and rhymes present stories which introduce numbers 0-10.
Subjects: LCSH Numeration—English--Dutch--Pictorial works--Juvenile literature. | BISAC JUVENILE NONFICTION /
Languages: English--Dutch
Classification: LCC QA141.3 .M57 2018 | DDC 513—dc23

Publisher: Lumpy Publishing
Website: www.missannabooks.com
Email: missanna@missannabooks.com

Paperback: ISBN 978-1-945977-42-8
Printed in the U.S.A.   1 3 5 7 9 10 8 6 4 2

Wil je onze nummer namen leren?

It is very easy and a lot of fun!

Het is heel gemakkelijk leuk!

Say-along our little jingle

Zing met ons me

starting from Number One!

beginnend met nummer één!

1

ONE looks like my one finger.

EEN

lijkt op mijn ene vinger.

ONE!
EEN!

2

TWO trails a tail.

TWEE

heeft een staart.

A TAIL! EEN STAART!

3

THREE   has bumps.

DRIE

heeft hobbels.

BUMPY!   HOBBELIG!

4
FOUR carries a sail.
VIER
draagt een zeil.

4
A SAIL!
EEN ZEIL!

5

FIVE is a racing track.

VIJF is een racebaan.

VROOM
VROOEEMM!
1

6

SIX curves like a snail.

ZES

is krom als een slak.

A SNAIL! EEN SLAK!

7

OUCH!
AUW!

8

EIGHT   is rollercoaster rails.

ACHT

is een achtbaan rails.

JIPPIE!
YIPPEE!

NINE   is a bubble on a stick.

NEGEN

is een bubbel op een stok.

A BUBBLE! EEN BUBBEL!

10

TEN is an eye of a whale.

TIEN

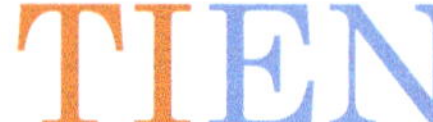

is één oog van een walvis.

WINK!
KNIPOOG!

And
En

0

ZERO   is an empty pail.

NUL

is een lege emmer.

IT'S
EMPTY!
Het is leeg!

Thank you for playing with us today.

We had a lot of fun too!

Bedankt dat je vandaag
met ons hebt gespeeld.
We hadden ook veel plezier!

We are your Number friends,
Zero to Ten,
Who will be here for you~
We zijn je nummer vrienden,
Nul tot Tien,
en we zullen er voor je zijn~

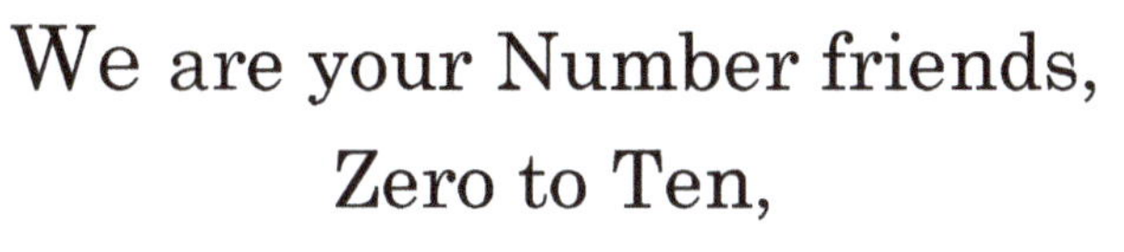

Bye-bye now!
See you again soon!
Tot ziens!
We zien je snel weer!

The Numbers are *SINGING* too!

To sing-a-long, look for Miss Anna Number Story
at your favorite music store like iTUNES.

MP3

Numbers 0-10
IDENTIFYING
& COUNTING

Numbers 11-20
& Ordinals

first, second, third...

Numbers 0-100
& Place Values

ones, tens, hundreds...

About Clocks
& Telling Time

hours, minutes, seconds

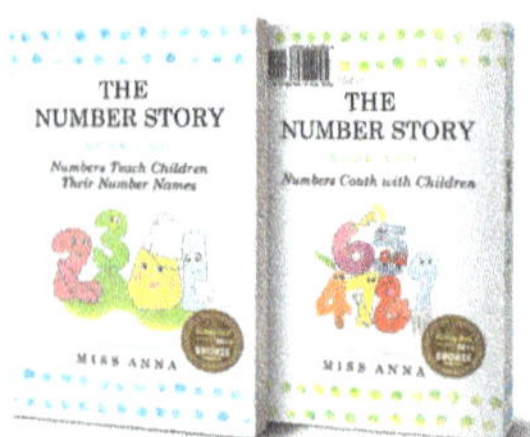

Number Story 1 & 2

isbn: 978-0-996216-48-7

Number Story 3 & 4

isbn: 978-1-945977-01-5

Number Story 5 & 6

isbn: 978-1-945977-06-0

Number Story 7 & 8

isbn: 978-1-949320-40-4

For more Miss Anna books to love,
visit us at

w w w . m i s s a n n a b o o k s . c o m

Numbers are working hard all over the world!
Come Travel the World with Us!